Evil Women in History: Uncovering the Gruesome Crimes of Ten Notorious Female Killers

While every precaution has been taken in the preparation of this book, the publisher assumes no responsibility for errors or omissions, or for damages resulting from the use of the information contained herein.

EVIL WOMEN IN HISTORY: UNCOVERING THE GRUESOME CRIMES OF TEN NOTORIOUS FEMALE KILLERS

First edition. July 8, 2023.

Copyright © 2023 Edward Turner.

ISBN: 979-8223278733

Written by Edward Turner.

Also by Edward Turner

Ghosts of Paris: Ten Haunted Places in the City of Love
Appalachian Nightmares: The Top 10 Creepy Creatures of the Mountains
Asia's Top Ten Cryptids: Legends, Sightings, and Theories
Evil Women in History: Uncovering the Gruesome Crimes of Ten Notorious Female Killers
Ghosts of London: Ten Haunted Places in The City
Ghosts of New York: Ten Haunted Places in The Big Apple
Missouri Nightmares: The Top 10 Chilling Legends
North America's Top Ten Cryptids: Legends, Sightings, and Theories

Introduction

The women listed in the book framework as the top ten most evil in history were chosen based on a number of factors, including the nature and scale of their crimes, their motivations, and their impact on history and society. Each of these women has been identified as having committed heinous acts that have caused great harm to others, and their legacies continue to haunt the collective consciousness of humanity.

One factor that led to these women being identified as the most evil in history is the sheer scale of their crimes. Many of them were responsible for the deaths of large numbers of people, either through their actions as rulers or through acts of violence and murder. For example, Queen Mary I of England is believed to have executed over 300 Protestants during her reign, while Elizabeth Bathory is alleged to have killed hundreds of young girls in order to bathe in their blood. The sheer number of victims involved in these cases is staggering, and it speaks to the level of depravity and cruelty exhibited by these women.

Another factor that led to these women being identified as the most evil in history is the nature of their crimes. Many of them committed acts that were particularly heinous or gruesome, such as Bathory's alleged blood baths or the cannibalistic practices of Katherine Knight. These acts were not only horrifying in their own right, but they also served as a means of exerting power and control over others.

Motivation is also a factor that played a role in the selection of these women as the most evil in history. In some cases, their crimes were committed for personal gain, such as Isabella of Castile's persecution of the Jews, which was motivated by her desire to consolidate power and wealth. In other cases, the motivation was rooted in a twisted sense of ideology or belief, such as Mary I's persecution of Protestants in order to preserve Catholicism as the dominant religion in England.

Finally, the impact that these women had on history and society also contributed to their identification as the most evil in history. Their actions often had far-reaching consequences that went beyond the immediate harm caused to their victims. For example, Belle Gunness's alleged murders contributed to a broader cultural anxiety around the safety of women, while Ilse Koch's role in the Holocaust helped to perpetuate Nazi atrocities and shape the course of World War II.

The women identified as the top ten most evil in history were chosen based on a number of factors, including the scale and nature of their crimes, their motivations, and their impact on history and society. While their legacies are undeniably dark and disturbing, their stories also serve as a reminder of the depths of human depravity and the importance of vigilance in preventing such atrocities from occurring in the future.

Queen Mary I

QUEEN MARY I OF ENGLAND, also known as "Bloody Mary," is infamous for her persecution of Protestants during her reign from 1553-1558. She was a devout Catholic and sought to restore Catholicism as the dominant religion in England, leading to the execution of over 300 Protestants. Many of her victims were burned at the stake, earning her the nickname "Bloody Mary."

Myra Hindley

MYRA HINDLEY WAS A British serial killer who, along with her partner Ian Brady, was responsible for the abduction, sexual assault, and murder of five children between 1963 and 1965. The couple became known as the "Moors Murderers" because they buried their victims on Saddleworth Moor near Manchester. Hindley was convicted of two murders and Brady of three, and they were both sentenced to life in prison.

Isabella of Castile

ISABELLA OF CASTILE was a queen of Spain who is known for her persecution of Jews and Muslims during the Spanish Inquisition. She and her husband, Ferdinand II of Aragon, sought to establish Catholicism as the dominant religion in Spain and expelled both Jews and Muslims from the country. Those who did not convert were subject to torture and execution.

Beverly Allitt

BEVERLY ALLITT WAS a British nurse who was convicted of murdering four children and attempting to murder nine others while working at Grantham and Kesteven Hospital in Lincolnshire in 1991. She used a variety of methods to harm her patients, including injecting them with insulin and suffocating them.

Belle Gunness

BELLE GUNNESS WAS AN American serial killer who operated in the late 19th and early 20th centuries. She is believed to have killed at least 14 people, including her two husbands, children, and suitors who answered her personal ads seeking marriage. She was known for luring her victims to her farm in Indiana, where she would kill and bury them.

Mary Ann Cotton

MARY ANN COTTON WAS an English serial killer who was convicted of murdering her husbands, lovers, and children using arsenic poisoning in the mid-19th century. She is believed to have killed up to 21 people, including 11 of her own children, in order to collect life insurance payouts.

Ilse Koch

ILSE KOCH WAS A NAZI concentration camp guard and wife of the commandant of Buchenwald concentration camp in Germany. She was known for her cruelty towards prisoners and her penchant for collecting tattooed human skin. She was later tried and convicted of war crimes and sentenced to life in prison.

Irma Grese

IRMA GRESE WAS A FEMALE SS guard at Auschwitz and Bergen-Belsen concentration camps during World War II. She was known for her brutality towards prisoners and was involved in selecting prisoners for the gas chambers. She was later tried and convicted of war crimes and sentenced to death.

Katherine Knight

KATHERINE KNIGHT IS an Australian woman who was convicted of murdering her partner in 2001. She is known for her particularly gruesome methods, including skinning her partner and cooking parts of his body with the intent to serve them to his children.

Elizabeth Bathory

ELIZABETH BATHORY WAS a Hungarian noblewoman who is believed to have killed hundreds of young girls in the late 16th and early 17th centuries. She was known for her cruelty towards her victims, including torture, mutilation, and murder. She was later imprisoned and died in captivity.

These women were chosen for their heinous crimes and their impact on history and society. Their actions have left a lasting legacy of fear and trauma, reminding us of the depths of human depravity and the need for justice and accountability.

EDWARD TURNER

Chapter 1: Queen Mary I

Her background and rise to power.

Queen Mary I, also known as Mary Tudor or Bloody Mary, was born on February 18, 1516, in Greenwich, England. She was the daughter of King Henry VIII and his first wife, Catherine of Aragon. Mary was the only surviving child of Henry and Catherine, as her siblings were either stillborn or died in infancy.

Mary's early life was marked by turmoil, as her parents' marriage was annulled by the Church of England when she was just two years old. This led to a bitter and protracted conflict between Henry VIII and the Catholic Church, as well as a strained relationship between Mary and her father. Henry remarried five more times, and Mary was declared illegitimate and removed from the line of succession.

Mary was raised in isolation, and her education focused on religion, Latin, and music. She was a devout Catholic and opposed her father's reforms of the Church of England, which included the establishment of the Anglican Church and the dissolution of monasteries.

In 1547, Henry VIII died, and Mary's half-brother Edward VI ascended to the throne. Edward was a Protestant and sought to continue his father's religious reforms. Mary, however, remained steadfast in her Catholic faith and was increasingly isolated during Edward's reign.

When Edward died in 1553, Mary seized the opportunity to claim the throne. She was supported by Catholic nobles and the Spanish ambassador, and she was able to gather an army to depose the Protestant Lady Jane Grey, who had been named queen by a faction of nobles after Edward's death.

Mary's reign began on July 19, 1553, and she immediately set about reversing her father's reforms and restoring Catholicism as the dominant religion in England. She repealed the laws that had established the Anglican Church, restored papal authority, and began to suppress Protestantism.

Mary's persecution of Protestants was brutal and systematic. She ordered the arrest and execution of Protestant leaders, burned Protestant books, and closed Protestant churches. Her reign was marked by the execution of over 300 Protestants, many of whom were burned at the stake. This earned her the nickname "Bloody Mary."

Mary's persecution of Protestants was not just driven by religious zeal; it was also a means of consolidating her power and asserting her authority. She faced opposition from Protestant nobles and foreign powers, particularly France, which supported the Protestant cause in England.

Mary's reign was also marked by political instability and economic hardship. Her marriage to Philip II of Spain, a staunch Catholic, was unpopular, and she faced several rebellions, including Wyatt's Rebellion in 1554. The economy suffered from a series of poor harvests and inflation, which led to social unrest.

Mary's reign came to an end with her death on November 17, 1558. She was succeeded by her half-sister, Elizabeth I, who was a Protestant and reversed many of Mary's policies. Mary's legacy is a controversial one; she is revered by Catholics as a defender of the faith, but reviled by Protestants for her persecution of their religion.

Mary's rise to power was a long and tumultuous journey that was marked by political intrigue, religious upheaval, and personal tragedy. Her ascent to the throne was not an easy one, as she faced opposition from both domestic and foreign forces, and had to overcome several obstacles to achieve her goal.

One of the key factors in Mary's rise to power was her royal lineage. She was the daughter of King Henry VIII, who was one of the most powerful monarchs in Europe at the time. Henry was notorious for his multiple marriages and his desire for a male heir, but he also had a strong interest in securing his dynasty and ensuring that his offspring would succeed him on the throne.

Mary was Henry's only surviving child from his first marriage to Catherine of Aragon, and as such, she had a strong claim to the throne. However, her legitimacy was called into question after her father's marriage to Anne Boleyn, who gave birth to Elizabeth I. Mary was declared illegitimate, and her status as a potential heir was thrown into doubt.

Despite this setback, Mary remained a prominent figure at court, and she was educated in a range of subjects, including music, languages, and religion. She was a devout Catholic, and her faith played a central role in her political outlook and her sense of identity.

When Henry died in 1547, Mary's half-brother Edward VI succeeded him to the throne. Edward was a staunch Protestant, and he sought to continue his father's reforms of the Church of England. Mary, however, remained a Catholic, and she became increasingly isolated during Edward's reign.

Mary's fortunes began to change when Edward fell ill and it became clear that he would not survive. The question of succession was a contentious one, as Edward had named his cousin, Lady Jane Grey, as his heir, bypassing both Mary and Elizabeth. Lady Jane's claim to the throne was supported by a faction of Protestant nobles, but Mary refused to accept her as queen.

Mary was able to gather support from Catholic nobles and from the Spanish ambassador, who was keen to see a Catholic monarch on the throne of England. She raised an army and marched on London, where she was declared queen on July 19, 1553.

Mary's ascension to the throne was not without its challenges, however. She faced opposition from both Protestant and Catholic factions, and she had to navigate a delicate political landscape to secure her position. She also faced a rebellion led by Sir Thomas Wyatt, which threatened to topple her regime.

Despite these challenges, Mary was able to consolidate her power and assert her authority as queen. She repealed the laws that had established the Church of England, restored papal authority, and began to suppress Protestantism. Her reign was marked by a series of religious and political upheavals, but she remained steadfast in her commitment to Catholicism and her belief in her divine right to rule.

Mary's rise to power was a testament to her determination and resilience. She faced numerous obstacles and setbacks, but she was able to overcome them through a combination of political skill, military might, and sheer force of will. Her legacy as a monarch may be controversial, but there is no denying the impact that she had on English history, and the enduring fascination that her story continues to hold for scholars and the public alike.

Her persecution of Protestants and executions.

ONE OF THE MOST CONTROVERSIAL aspects of Queen Mary I's reign was her persecution of Protestants, which included a series of executions and burnings that have come to be known as the Marian Persecutions.

Mary was a devout Catholic, and she believed that it was her duty to restore the Catholic Church in England. She saw Protestantism as a threat to the religious and political stability of the realm, and she was determined to stamp it out.

One of the first steps that Mary took was to repeal the laws that had established the Church of England under her father, Henry VIII, and her half-brother, Edward VI. She restored papal authority and began to reinstate Catholic practices, such as the use of Latin in the liturgy and the veneration of saints.

These moves were met with resistance from many Protestants, who saw them as an attack on their faith and their liberty. Mary responded by passing a series of laws that made it a crime to deny the real presence of Christ in the Eucharist, to question the authority of the pope, or to attend Protestant services.

These laws were enforced by a network of informants, spies, and inquisitors, who were tasked with identifying and prosecuting anyone who was suspected of heresy. Many Protestants went into hiding or fled the country, but others were captured and put on trial.

The most famous of these trials was that of Archbishop Thomas Cranmer, who had been one of the architects of the English Reformation. Cranmer was arrested in 1553 and brought before a court on charges of heresy. He initially recanted his Protestant beliefs, but he later retracted his confession and was burned at the stake in 1556.

Cranmer was not the only prominent Protestant to suffer this fate. Other notable victims of the Marian Persecutions included bishops Hugh Latimer and Nicholas Ridley, who were burned together in Oxford in 1555, and the scholar and preacher John Bradford, who was burned in London in the same year.

In total, it is estimated that around 300 Protestants were executed during Mary's reign, although the exact number is difficult to determine. The burnings were often carried out in public, and they were intended to serve as a warning to others who might be tempted to dissent from the Catholic faith.

The Marian Persecutions have been the subject of much debate and controversy over the years. Some historians argue that Mary was simply a product of her time, and that the persecution of heretics was a common practice throughout Europe in the sixteenth century. Others see her as a fanatical and tyrannical ruler, who was willing to sacrifice the lives of her subjects in pursuit of her religious agenda.

Whatever one's opinion of Mary's actions, there is no doubt that her persecution of Protestants had a profound impact on English history. It helped to deepen the religious divisions that would eventually lead to the Civil War, and it left a lasting legacy of fear and suspicion that would haunt the nation for centuries to come.

Her legacy and impact on England

QUEEN MARY I, ALSO known as Mary Tudor, left a complex legacy and had a significant impact on England during her brief reign. While she is often remembered for her persecution of Protestants, her policies also had a lasting impact on the country's religious and political landscape.

One of Mary's most enduring legacies was the restoration of the Catholic Church in England. During her reign, she reversed the religious reforms of her father, Henry VIII, and her half-brother, Edward VI, and re-established papal authority. She also worked to restore Catholic practices, such as the use of Latin in the liturgy, the veneration of saints, and the celebration of Mass.

This restoration of Catholicism had a significant impact on English society. It marked a clear break from the religious and political reforms of the previous decades, and it helped to deepen the divide between Catholics and Protestants in England. This divide would eventually lead to the Civil War, which had a profound impact on the country's political and social landscape.

Another aspect of Mary's legacy was her marriage to Philip II of Spain. Mary's marriage to Philip was controversial, and it sparked fears that England would become a vassal state of Spain. However, the marriage had important political and economic implications. It helped to secure England's position as a major European power and facilitated trade and commerce between the two countries.

Mary's reign also saw the introduction of a number of important legal and administrative reforms. She re-established the Court of Star Chamber, which was a key institution for maintaining law and order in England. She also introduced new regulations for the wool trade, which was a major source of wealth for the country at the time.

Despite these achievements, Mary is primarily remembered for her persecution of Protestants. The Marian Persecutions, as they came to be known, were a series of executions and burnings that were carried out against those who refused to renounce their Protestant beliefs. These persecutions were brutal and caused a great deal of fear and tension within the country.

The legacy of the Marian Persecutions has been the subject of much debate and controversy over the years. While some argue that Mary was simply a product of her time and that the persecution of heretics was common practice throughout Europe in the sixteenth century, others see her as a fanatical and tyrannical ruler who was willing to sacrifice the lives of her subjects in pursuit of her religious agenda.

Despite the controversy surrounding her reign, Mary's impact on England was profound. Her policies helped to shape the religious and political landscape of the country, and her legacy can still be felt today. While she may have been a controversial figure, there is no doubt that Mary Tudor left a lasting mark on English history.

EDWARD TURNER

16

Chapter 2: Myra Hindley

Her background and relationship with Ian Brady

Myra Hindley was born on July 23, 1942, in Manchester, England. She was the eldest of two children and grew up in a working-class family. Her parents were often fighting, and her father was an alcoholic who would regularly physically and emotionally abuse Hindley and her mother.

Despite the chaos in her family life, Hindley was a bright student and excelled academically. She attended Ryder Brow Secondary Modern School, where she was known for being a diligent student. However, she struggled to make friends and was often bullied by her classmates. Her difficult childhood and lack of social skills may have contributed to her later involvement in criminal activities.

In 1961, Hindley was working as a typist at the same company as Ian Brady, a young man who had a fascination with Nazi Germany and a dark obsession with sadism and violence. The two became friends, and their relationship soon turned romantic. Hindley was completely enamored with Brady, and the two shared a deep bond based on their shared fascination with death and violence.

Brady introduced Hindley to his twisted world, showing her photographs and books about Nazi concentration camps and sharing his fantasies about committing violent crimes. Hindley quickly became infatuated with Brady's sadistic tendencies, and she became his willing accomplice in a series of brutal murders that would terrorize England for years to come.

Together, Hindley and Brady would go on to commit the infamous Moors Murders. They abducted, sexually assaulted, and murdered five children and teenagers between 1963 and 1965. The couple would take their victims to remote locations, often on Saddleworth Moor, where they would be brutally tortured, raped, and murdered.

Hindley played an active role in these murders. She would help Brady lure victims to their car, and she would sometimes participate in the assaults and murders. In one particularly shocking case, Hindley photographed Brady sexually assaulting 10-year-old Lesley Ann Downey before the girl was killed.

It wasn't until Hindley's brother-in-law, David Smith, went to the police and confessed to helping Brady and Hindley dispose of a body that the couple's reign of terror was finally brought to an end. The police were able to connect Hindley and Brady to the murders, and both were arrested in October 1965.

Hindley initially denied any involvement in the murders, but she eventually confessed and led police to the graves of their victims. At their trial, Hindley and Brady were both found guilty of murder and sentenced to life in prison.

Hindley spent the rest of her life in prison, becoming one of the most infamous female criminals in British history. Her relationship with Brady and her role in the Moors Murders continue to fascinate and horrify the public, and her name has become synonymous with evil.

Myra Hindley's background as a troubled, lonely child and her later infatuation with Ian Brady's dark obsessions led her down a path of evil and violence. Her involvement in the Moors Murders cemented her place as one of the most notorious criminals in British history.

The murders of children and cover-up

THE MURDERS COMMITTED by Myra Hindley and Ian Brady are some of the most heinous in British history. The pair is believed to have killed at least five children between July 1963 and October 1965. The victims were all young and vulnerable, and the nature of the crimes shook the nation to its core.

Hindley and Brady's first victim was Pauline Reade, a 16-year-old girl whom Hindley had befriended at her place of work. On the 12th of July 1963, Hindley asked Pauline to help her locate a lost glove on Saddleworth Moor. Brady was waiting nearby, and when Pauline arrived, he attacked her, sexually assaulted her, and then murdered her. Hindley was complicit in the crime and helped to dispose of the body.

Their second victim was John Kilbride, a 12-year-old boy who they lured into their car outside a market in Ashton-under-Lyne. Brady sexually assaulted and murdered him on the same moor where they had killed Pauline Reade.

The pair's third victim was Keith Bennett, a 12-year-old boy whom they snatched from a street in Manchester. They drove him to Saddleworth Moor, where they sexually assaulted him and buried his body. To this day, Keith's remains have not been found.

Their fourth victim was Lesley Ann Downey, a 10-year-old girl whom they lured away from a funfair in Greater Manchester. They took her back to Hindley's house, where they subjected her to a horrific ordeal of sexual abuse, torture, and murder. They recorded some of the torture on audiotape, and the sounds of Lesley Ann's screams still haunt those who have heard them.

The final victim was Edward Evans, a 17-year-old boy who Brady had met in Manchester. On the 6th of October 1965, Brady invited Evans to Hindley's house, where he murdered him with an axe. The murder was witnessed by Hindley's brother-in-law, David Smith, who subsequently went to the police.

The murders were discovered when the police found the body of Edward Evans in Hindley's house. They then found incriminating evidence, including photographs and tapes of the other victims, at Brady and Hindley's homes. The pair was arrested and charged with murder, and their trial began on the 19th of April 1966.

At the trial, the prosecution presented a case that was based largely on the testimony of David Smith, who had agreed to give evidence in exchange for immunity. He described in detail the murder of Edward Evans and the involvement of Hindley and Brady in the other murders.

Hindley and Brady were both found guilty of murder and sentenced to life imprisonment. Hindley died in prison in 2002, while Brady died in 2017. The case remains one of the most notorious in British criminal history, and the brutality of the crimes has left an indelible mark on the nation's psyche.

Her trial and imprisonment

MYRA HINDLEY AND IAN Brady's trial was one of the most highly publicized and shocking cases in British legal history. After being arrested in October 1965, Hindley was charged with the murders of Edward Evans, Lesley Ann Downey, and John Kilbride. Brady was charged with the murders of John Kilbride, Lesley Ann Downey, and Edward Evans, as well as the murder of 17-year-old Edward Evans. The trial began on April 19, 1966, and lasted for 14 days.

At the trial, the prosecution presented a wealth of evidence against the couple, including tape recordings of Lesley Ann Downey's screams as she was being tortured and killed, as well as photographs taken by Hindley of their victims. The prosecution also presented evidence that Hindley had taken part in the murder of Edward Evans, which Hindley initially denied.

The defense team attempted to portray Hindley as a victim of Brady's manipulation, arguing that she was not responsible for her actions. However, this defense was largely unsuccessful, and both Hindley and Brady were found guilty of all the charges against them. The judge, Mr. Justice Fenton Atkinson, sentenced them both to life imprisonment, with a recommendation that they should never be released.

Hindley's imprisonment was controversial, with some arguing that she had been unfairly demonized by the media and that her role in the murders had been overstated. However, her continued refusal to take responsibility for her actions and her lack of remorse made it difficult for many to sympathize with her.

In 1987, Hindley made a full confession to the police, admitting to her role in the murders and implicating Brady in the killing of Keith Bennett, whose body had never been found. This confession led to renewed interest in the case, and there were calls for Hindley's release, as she had now accepted responsibility for her crimes. However, the families of the victims, along with many others, vehemently opposed her release, and she remained in prison until her death in 2002.

Hindley's imprisonment and the ongoing debate about her role in the murders continue to be the subject of intense scrutiny and controversy in Britain. Her case has raised important questions about the nature of evil, the possibility of redemption, and the limits of human compassion. While some may argue that Hindley was a victim of circumstance or of Brady's manipulation, others maintain that she was a willing participant in some of the most heinous crimes in British history and that her actions cannot be excused or forgiven.

Chapter 3: Isabella of Castile

Her background and reign as queen

Isabella of Castile, also known as Isabella I or Isabel la Católica, was a queen of Castile and Leon from 1474 to 1504. She was born in Madrigal de las Altas Torres, Castile, on April 22, 1451, to King John II of Castile and his second wife, Isabella of Portugal. She was the second child of the couple and was educated in religion and politics from an early age.

As a young princess, Isabella faced numerous challenges, including the conflict between her father and her half-brother, Henry IV of Castile. Henry IV was seen by many as a weak ruler and was accused of being impotent, which led to doubts about the legitimacy of his daughter Joanna "la Beltraneja" as his heir. Isabella was considered a more suitable heir by many, and after the death of her half-brother in 1474, she became queen of Castile and Leon.

Isabella's reign was marked by a series of achievements, including the completion of the Reconquista, the expulsion of Jews and Muslims from Spain, and the beginning of Spain's exploration and colonization of the Americas. Isabella was also known for her patronage of the arts and for her support of Christopher Columbus, who made his famous voyage across the Atlantic under her sponsorship.

Under Isabella's rule, Spain became a more centralized and powerful nation, with a strong monarchy and a unified national identity. However, her reign was also marked by controversy, particularly with regard to her treatment of non-Catholics. In 1492, she issued the Alhambra Decree, which ordered the expulsion of all Jews from Spain. This decree was seen by many as an act of religious intolerance and persecution.

Despite these controversies, Isabella is still widely regarded as one of the most important monarchs in Spanish history. Her reign marked a significant turning point in the history of Spain and Europe, and her legacy continues to be felt today.

Isabella married Ferdinand II of Aragon in 1469, and the couple ruled Spain together as joint monarchs. This marriage was a crucial political alliance, as it brought together the two most powerful kingdoms in Spain and paved the way for the unification of the country. Isabella and Ferdinand had five children, including Joanna the Mad and Catherine of Aragon, who would later become the queen of England as the first wife of King Henry VIII.

As queen, Isabella was known for her piety and her strong Catholic faith. She was a devout believer and was deeply committed to the Catholic Church, which had a significant influence on her policies and decisions. Isabella was also known for her intelligence and her political acumen, which helped her to navigate the complex political landscape of late medieval Spain.

Throughout her reign, Isabella faced numerous challenges, including rebellion and resistance from some of her subjects. However, she was able to overcome these challenges through a combination of military force, diplomacy, and cunning. She was also known for her generosity and her concern for the welfare of her people, which earned her the nickname "the Catholic."

Isabella's reign was marked by a series of achievements, including the completion of the Reconquista, the campaign to drive the Muslim Moors out of Spain. This was a major military campaign that lasted for centuries, and Isabella's victory marked the end of Muslim rule in Spain. She was also a patron of the arts, and under her sponsorship, Spanish literature, architecture, and painting flourished.

Perhaps Isabella's most famous achievement was her sponsorship of Christopher Columbus's voyage to the Americas in 1492. Columbus had been seeking sponsorship for his voyage for several years, but had been rejected by numerous monarchs and officials. Isabella, however, was intrigued by his proposal and saw it as an opportunity to spread Christianity and expand Spanish influence across the Atlantic. She provided him with funding, ships, and supplies, and he set off on his famous voyage under her sponsorship. This journey ultimately led to the discovery of the New World and the beginning of Spain's colonization of the Americas.

However, Isabella's reign was also marked by controversy and criticism, particularly with regard to her treatment of non-Catholics. In 1478, she established the Spanish

Inquisition, which was tasked with rooting out heresy and enforcing religious conformity. This led to the persecution of thousands of Jews and Muslims, who were forced to convert to Christianity or face exile or execution. The Inquisition was also used to suppress political dissent, and many individuals were accused of heresy for political reasons.

Perhaps the most infamous act of Isabella's reign was the expulsion of the Jews from Spain in 1492. This decree ordered all Jews to convert to Christianity or leave the country within four months. Those who refused to leave or convert were subject to imprisonment, torture, and death. The decree was a culmination of years of anti-Semitic sentiment in Spain and was seen by many as an act of religious intolerance and persecution.

Despite these controversies, Isabella's legacy is still celebrated in Spain and beyond. She is regarded as a strong and influential monarch who helped to shape the course of European history. Her reign marked the beginning of Spain's golden age, a period of cultural, economic, and political growth that lasted for centuries. Her support for Columbus's voyage to the Americas also had far-reaching consequences, including the establishment of the Spanish Empire and the spread of Christianity across the New World.

Isabella died on November 26, 1504, at the age of 53. Her reign had been marked by both triumphs and controversies, but her legacy as one of the most important monarchs in Spanish history endures. She is remembered as a devout Catholic, a patron of the arts, and a powerful ruler who helped to shape the course of European history. Her reign marked a turning point in the history of Spain and Europe, and her influence can still be felt today.

The expulsion of Jews and Muslims from Spain

THE EXPULSION OF JEWS and Muslims from Spain is one of the most significant events that occurred during Isabella of Castile's reign. This event is known as the Alhambra Decree or the Edict of Expulsion, and it was signed by Isabella and her husband, King Ferdinand II of Aragon, on March 31, 1492.

The decree ordered the expulsion of all Jews who refused to convert to Christianity from the Kingdom of Spain, including the recently conquered territories of Granada and Navarre. The decree also gave Jews a deadline of four months to leave the country or face execution. The edict was enforced with great cruelty and resulted in the forced conversion of many Jews and Muslims.

The reasons for the expulsion of the Jews and Muslims from Spain are complex, and there were several factors that contributed to it. One of the primary reasons was religious intolerance. The Catholic Church had been pushing for the expulsion of Jews and Muslims from Spain for several years, and Isabella was a devout Catholic who believed that the Jews and Muslims were a threat to the unity of Spain.

Another factor was economic. The Jewish and Muslim populations were among the wealthiest and most influential in Spain, and many Christians resented their success. Some Christians believed that the Jews and Muslims were using their wealth to gain power and influence over the Christian population.

The expulsion of the Jews and Muslims had a significant impact on Spain. It led to a decline in the country's economy and cultural diversity. Many of the Jews who were expelled were skilled craftsmen, merchants, and bankers, and their departure had a negative impact on Spain's economy.

The expulsion also had a significant impact on the Jewish community. Many Jews who refused to convert were forced to flee Spain, and they faced persecution and discrimination wherever they went. The event is still remembered by Jews today as a tragic and traumatic moment in their history.

Isabella's role in the expulsion of the Jews and Muslims from Spain has been a subject of controversy for centuries. Some historians argue that Isabella was merely following the Catholic Church's orders and that her role in the expulsion was minimal. Others argue that Isabella was a driving force behind the edict and that she was motivated by religious zeal and a desire to consolidate power.

Regardless of Isabella's exact role, the expulsion of the Jews and Muslims from Spain was a tragic event that had a lasting impact on Spain and the Jewish community. It remains a controversial and divisive topic to this day.

Her role in the Spanish Inquisition

ONE OF THE MOST CONTROVERSIAL aspects of Isabella's reign was her role in the Spanish Inquisition. The Inquisition was established in 1478 by Isabella and her husband Ferdinand in order to root out heresy and maintain religious unity in Spain. The Inquisition was initially established as a joint effort between the Spanish monarchy and the Catholic Church, but it was ultimately controlled by the monarchy.

The Inquisition was responsible for investigating and punishing individuals who were suspected of heresy, including Jews, Muslims, and conversos, or Jews and Muslims who had converted to Christianity. The Inquisition was notorious for its harsh methods of interrogation and punishment, including torture and execution. Many people were falsely accused of heresy and subjected to the Inquisition's brutal methods, and the Inquisition became a symbol of religious intolerance and persecution.

Isabella's role in the Inquisition was controversial and has been debated by historians for centuries. Some historians argue that Isabella was motivated by a sincere desire to maintain religious unity in Spain, while others see her as a ruthless monarch who used the Inquisition as a tool of political power.

There is no doubt that Isabella was deeply committed to the Catholic Church and saw herself as a defender of the faith. She believed that the Inquisition was necessary to protect the purity of the Catholic faith and to root out heresy and corruption. She also saw the Inquisition as a way to demonstrate her piety and her commitment to the Catholic Church.

Isabella was closely involved in the establishment of the Inquisition and played an active role in its operations. She appointed the first inquisitors and provided them with funding and resources. She also issued several edicts and decrees that expanded the scope and power of the Inquisition.

One of the most controversial aspects of Isabella's involvement in the Inquisition was her role in the expulsion of the Jews from Spain. In 1492, Isabella and Ferdinand issued the Alhambra Decree, which ordered the expulsion of all Jews from Spain. This decree was motivated in part by religious reasons, as Isabella believed that the Jews were responsible for the death of Christ and were a threat to the purity of the Catholic faith. However, the expulsion of the Jews was also motivated by political and economic factors, as many of the Jews in Spain were wealthy and successful.

The expulsion of the Jews from Spain was a traumatic event that had a profound impact on Jewish communities throughout Europe. Many Jews were forced to leave their homes and possessions behind and were subjected to violence and persecution. The expulsion also had a significant economic impact on Spain, as the Jews had played an important role in the country's commerce and industry.

Isabella's involvement in the Inquisition remains a controversial and divisive issue. Some historians see her as a devout and pious queen who was committed to the Catholic faith, while others see her as a ruthless monarch who used the Inquisition as a tool of political power. Regardless of one's opinion of Isabella, there is no denying that her reign had a profound impact on Spain and on European history as a whole. Her legacy continues to be felt today, both in Spain and throughout the world.

EDWARD TURNER

Chapter 4: Beverly Allitt

Her background and employment as a nurse

Beverly Allitt is a British serial killer who was convicted of murdering four children and attempting to murder nine others while working as a pediatric nurse in the early 1990s. Allitt was born on October 4, 1968, in Grantham, Lincolnshire, England. She grew up in a working-class family and was described as a quiet and introverted child. Her parents divorced when she was young, and she lived with her mother and stepfather for most of her childhood.

Allitt was interested in nursing from a young age and began training as a nurse at Grantham and Kesteven Hospital in 1987. She qualified as a State Enrolled Nurse (SEN) in 1991 and began working as a pediatric nurse at Grantham and Kesteven Hospital. Allitt was described as a competent and caring nurse, and she quickly became a popular member of the hospital staff.

However, Allitt's behavior began to change in early 1991, when she started to make a series of bizarre and disturbing comments to her colleagues. She also began to exhibit strange behavior, such as injecting herself with insulin in front of her colleagues and stealing drugs from the hospital's pharmacy. Despite these warning signs, Allitt was allowed to continue working as a nurse.

Over a period of just 59 days between February and April 1991, Allitt killed four children and attempted to murder nine others while working as a pediatric nurse. Her victims were all under the age of five and were suffering from a range of illnesses and conditions. Allitt's first victim was a two-month-old baby named Liam Taylor, who died of heart failure after Allitt injected him with a large dose of insulin. Over the next few weeks, Allitt continued to kill and injure children, using a variety of methods including injections, suffocation, and smothering.

Allitt's crimes were discovered after a pattern of unexplained deaths and illnesses among the children in her care was noticed by hospital staff. Suspicion eventually fell on Allitt, and she was arrested in April 1991. During her trial, Allitt denied any wrongdoing and claimed that her actions were due to a psychiatric condition. However, she was found guilty of four counts of murder, three counts of attempted murder, and six counts of causing grievous bodily harm with intent.

Allitt was sentenced to life imprisonment with a minimum term of 30 years, making her one of the few women in British history to receive a whole-life tariff. She was diagnosed with Munchausen syndrome by proxy, a rare psychological disorder in which a caregiver causes or fabricates illness in a person under their care in order to gain attention or sympathy. Allitt's motive for her crimes remains unclear, but it is believed that she may have been seeking attention or sympathy from her colleagues and patients.

Allitt's crimes shocked the British public and led to calls for greater scrutiny of nurses and other healthcare professionals. The case also highlighted the need for improved training and support for healthcare workers who are dealing with difficult and stressful situations on a daily basis.

In the years since her conviction, Allitt has remained in prison and has reportedly shown little remorse for her crimes. Her case continues to be studied by criminologists and psychologists, who are seeking to understand the factors that led to her shocking crimes. Allitt's case also serves as a reminder of the dangers of Munchausen syndrome by proxy and the need for greater awareness and understanding of this rare but devastating disorder.

The poisoning and murder of children

BEVERLY ALLITT'S CRIMES revolved around poisoning and murder of children. Allitt worked as a pediatric nurse at the Grantham and Kesteven Hospital in Lincolnshire, England, from 1991 to 1993. During her employment, Allitt became known for her friendly demeanor and her seemingly caring attitude toward her young patients. However, beneath this facade, Allitt was harboring dark and twisted desires.

Allitt's crimes began in February 1991 when a child under her care suffered a sudden and unexplained collapse. The child, who was just seven weeks old, had been admitted to the hospital with breathing difficulties but was otherwise healthy. Allitt administered an injection to the child, and soon afterward, the child's breathing became shallow, and the infant lost consciousness. Despite the best efforts of the hospital staff, the child died a short time later.

Over the next few months, more children under Allitt's care began to experience similar unexplained collapses. Some children recovered, while others did not. Allitt's colleagues became suspicious of her, but it wasn't until March 1991 that she was caught in the act of attempting to poison a child. Allitt had injected the child with a large dose of insulin, causing the child's blood sugar levels to drop dangerously low. Fortunately, the child was discovered in time, and Allitt was arrested.

Further investigations revealed that Allitt had committed numerous acts of deliberate harm against children in her care. She had administered overdoses of insulin, potassium, and other drugs, causing some children to go into cardiac arrest and others to suffer brain damage. In total, Allitt was responsible for the deaths of four children and the serious injury of nine others.

Allitt's motives for her crimes remain unclear, although some speculate that she may have been motivated by a desire for attention or by a twisted desire to play the role of a savior, rescuing children from the brink of death. Whatever her motives, Allitt's crimes represent one of the most shocking and disturbing cases of medical malpractice in recent history.

The impact of Allitt's crimes on the families of the victims was devastating. The parents of the children who died or were seriously injured were left with a deep sense of grief and loss. Many felt that they had failed to protect their children, and some even blamed themselves for not realizing sooner that something was wrong.

Allitt's crimes also had a profound impact on the medical community in the UK. The case led to increased scrutiny of the hiring practices and training of nurses and other medical staff. Hospitals across the country introduced new measures to prevent similar tragedies from occurring in the future.

Allitt was eventually found guilty of murder and attempted murder and was sentenced to life imprisonment. She is currently serving her sentence at Rampton Secure Hospital, a high-security psychiatric facility in Nottinghamshire, England. Allitt's crimes continue to be studied and analyzed by criminologists and medical professionals, as a cautionary tale about the dangers of medical malpractice and the importance of vigilant oversight and regulation of healthcare professionals.

Her arrest, trial, and imprisonment

AFTER MONTHS OF INVESTIGATION, Beverly Allitt was arrested on May 21, 1993, and charged with four counts of murder and 11 counts of attempted murder. The trial began on February 1, 1993, and lasted for three months. The prosecution presented evidence that Allitt had deliberately poisoned her patients with insulin, potassium chloride, and other drugs.

The trial was one of the most high-profile criminal cases in British history, and it attracted intense media attention. Allitt was portrayed in the press as a cold and calculating killer, and her actions were seen as particularly heinous because they targeted vulnerable and defenseless children.

During the trial, Allitt maintained her innocence and claimed that she had been wrongly accused. However, the evidence presented against her was overwhelming, and the jury found her guilty on all charges. She was sentenced to life imprisonment with a minimum term of 30 years, making her one of the few women in British history to receive such a severe sentence.

Allitt's crimes had a profound impact on the families of her victims and on the wider community. The public was horrified by the thought that a nurse, someone who was supposed to care for the sick and vulnerable, could deliberately harm and kill children in her care.

The case also led to a review of nursing practices in the UK, with the government introducing stricter regulations and training requirements for nurses. The case highlighted the need for greater oversight and monitoring of healthcare professionals, and it led to increased scrutiny of the conduct of medical professionals.

After her conviction, Allitt was sent to Rampton Secure Hospital, a high-security psychiatric facility in Nottinghamshire. She was diagnosed with Munchausen syndrome by proxy, a psychological disorder in which a caregiver intentionally harms someone under their care in order to gain attention or sympathy.

Allitt's imprisonment has been marked by controversy, with some arguing that her sentence is too harsh given her mental health issues. However, the families of her victims have been vocal in their support of the sentence, arguing that Allitt's crimes were premeditated and deliberate, and that she should never be released.

In 2018, it was reported that Allitt had been moved to a less secure facility, sparking outrage among the families of her victims. They argued that Allitt still posed a danger to society and that she should never be allowed to leave prison.

Beverly Allitt's crimes shocked and horrified the world. Her deliberate poisoning and murder of innocent children represents one of the most heinous crimes in modern British history. While her motive for committing these crimes remains unclear, the impact of her actions on the families of her victims and on society as a whole cannot be overstated. Her trial and imprisonment serve as a stark reminder of the need for vigilance and oversight in the medical profession and of the devastating consequences that can result when healthcare professionals abuse their position of trust.

40

Chapter 5: Belle Gunness

Her background and multiple marriages

Belle Gunness was a notorious American serial killer who operated in the early 20th century. She is believed to have killed numerous men, women, and children, possibly including her own children, before disappearing in 1908. Gunness's true number of victims remains unknown, but she is suspected of killing at least 14 people, including two husbands and several suitors who answered her personal ads in newspapers.

Gunness was born in Selbu, Norway, on November 11, 1859, as Brynhild Paulsdatter Størseth. She immigrated to the United States in 1881, settling in Chicago. There, she met and married Mads Albert Sorenson, a fellow Norwegian immigrant, in 1884. The couple had four children together, but only one, a daughter named Caroline, survived past infancy. The other three children died under suspicious circumstances, with Gunness being suspected of poisoning them.

Gunness's first husband died in 1900, under similarly suspicious circumstances. After collecting a sizable life insurance payout, she began placing ads in newspapers seeking wealthy suitors. Over the next several years, she corresponded with numerous men and women who responded to her ads, many of whom eventually visited her farm in La Porte, Indiana.

It is believed that Gunness lured her victims to her farm with promises of love, marriage, and financial stability. Once they arrived, she would poison them or bludgeon them to death with a meat cleaver, before dismembering their bodies and burying them on her property. She was particularly known for her skill at dismemberment, and some of her victims' bodies were never found or only found in parts.

In 1908, a fire broke out at Gunness's farm, and the bodies of her two children and an unknown woman were found in the ruins. Gunness was initially believed to have died in the fire as well, but suspicions were raised when several of her suitors reported that they had received letters from her after the fire had occurred. In response, authorities began digging up the property, where they found the remains of at least 12 more people, including Gunness's first husband and several suitors.

Despite widespread suspicion that Gunness was still alive and on the run, she was never captured, and her ultimate fate remains a mystery. Some have speculated that she faked her own death and went on to live under a different identity, while others believe that she was killed by an accomplice or a vengeful victim's family member.

Gunness's crimes were particularly shocking and sensationalized at the time, not only because of their brutality but also because they challenged societal norms about women's roles and behaviors. Gunness was a striking figure who was known for her height and strength, as well as her apparent disregard for social conventions and traditional gender roles. Her crimes were seen as a stark departure from the typical behavior of women at the time, and many found it difficult to reconcile the idea of a female serial killer with their preconceived notions of femininity.

In the years since Gunness's crimes, she has become something of a cultural icon, inspiring numerous books, articles, and films. She has also been the subject of much speculation and myth-making, with some believing that she was a prolific killer responsible for far more deaths than can be confirmed, and others casting her as a victim of circumstances beyond her control. Regardless of the interpretation, Gunness's story remains a chilling reminder of the dark and complex nature of human behavior, and a cautionary tale about the dangers of unchecked ambition and greed.

The murders of husbands and suitors for financial gain

BELLE GUNNESS WAS A Norwegian-born American serial killer who became notorious for murdering her husbands and suitors for financial gain. Born in Selbu, Norway in 1859, Belle immigrated to the United States in 1881 and settled in Chicago, Illinois. She was married twice and had four children, but all of them died under mysterious circumstances. Belle moved to La Porte, Indiana in 1901 and purchased a farm which would become the site of her gruesome crimes.

Belle's modus operandi was to place ads in newspapers seeking wealthy suitors, often claiming to be a wealthy widow seeking a new husband. She would then lure the suitors to her farm and murder them, often by poisoning them with strychnine.

She would then bury the bodies on her property, sometimes dismembering them first to make identification more difficult.

The true number of Belle's victims is unknown, but it is believed to be at least 14, and possibly as many as 40. Some of her victims were her husbands, while others were suitors who had responded to her newspaper ads. Belle was able to get away with her crimes for several years, as she was a skilled liar and manipulator. She was also able to cover up her crimes by burning down her house and claiming that she and her children had perished in the fire.

However, Belle's luck eventually ran out. In 1908, a farmhand who had worked for Belle reported her suspicious behavior to the authorities. Investigators searched her property and found the remains of several of her victims, including those of her last husband, Peter Gunness, and his two children. Belle herself was not found, leading to speculation that she had faked her own death and gone into hiding.

Despite numerous sightings and rumors over the years, Belle Gunness was never captured or definitively identified after her disappearance. The case has become a legend in American true crime history, with many theories and speculation about what may have happened to Belle and whether she was responsible for other unsolved crimes.

Belle Gunness's murders were motivated by financial gain, as she was able to collect large sums of money from her victims' estates. She was able to manipulate her suitors into giving her money, and she also committed insurance fraud by taking out policies on her husbands and then murdering them for the payouts.

The case of Belle Gunness highlights the dangers of online dating and the ease with which people can misrepresent themselves in order to deceive and manipulate others. It also raises questions about the justice system and the difficulties of catching serial killers, particularly in the era before modern forensic science and DNA analysis.

Belle Gunness's crimes have been the subject of numerous books, films, and television shows. She has been portrayed as a cold-blooded killer, a victim of circumstance, and everything in between. Despite the passage of over a century since her crimes, the case of Belle Gunness continues to fascinate and terrify people today.

Her disappearance and possible escape

THE DISAPPEARANCE OF Belle Gunness remains one of the most intriguing mysteries in American criminal history. Her story is filled with questions, including whether she actually died in a house fire or whether she faked her own death to escape capture.

Belle Gunness was born Brynhild Paulsdatter Størseth in Norway in 1859. She immigrated to the United States in 1881 and settled in Chicago, where she worked as a servant and eventually opened her own candy store. Belle married Mads Albert Sorenson in 1884, and the couple had four children together. However, tragedy struck when two of their children died under suspicious circumstances. Belle's husband also died in 1900, reportedly of heart failure.

After her husband's death, Belle collected a substantial life insurance payout, which she used to purchase a farm in La Porte, Indiana. There, she met and married Peter Gunness, a local butcher, in 1902. However, Peter died under mysterious circumstances in 1908, leaving Belle once again with a large insurance payout.

It was at this point that Belle's murders began in earnest. She placed ads in newspapers seeking wealthy suitors, and then lured them to her farm under false pretenses. Once they were there, she drugged and killed them, then buried their bodies on her property. Over the next few years, she is believed to have killed at least 14 people, including her own children.

Belle's reign of terror came to an end in April 1908, when a fire broke out at her farmhouse. When firefighters arrived, they discovered the bodies of Belle's three children, as well as the body of a woman who was believed to be Belle herself. However, the head and hands of the woman were missing, leading some to speculate that the body had been planted to cover Belle's escape.

Over the years, numerous theories have been proposed about what really happened to Belle Gunness. Some believe that she faked her own death and escaped, possibly to start a new life under a new identity. Others speculate that she was killed by one of her accomplices, who then burned down the farmhouse to cover up the crime. Still, others believe that Belle's body was never found, and that she may have been responsible for even more murders than were initially suspected.

In 1931, a woman named Esther Carlson was arrested for poisoning a man and his daughter with strychnine. While in police custody, Carlson confessed to being Belle Gunness and claimed that she had faked her own death and fled to California. However, many people remained skeptical of Carlson's story, and it is unclear whether she was actually Belle Gunness or simply a disturbed woman seeking attention.

Despite the numerous theories and speculations, the truth about Belle Gunness's disappearance remains a mystery. Her story continues to captivate people today, and she is remembered as one of the most infamous female serial killers in American history.

EDWARD TURNER

48

Chapter 6: Mary Ann Cotton

Her background and marriages

Mary Ann Cotton was an English serial killer who murdered her victims by poisoning them with arsenic. She is believed to have killed up to 21 people, including her husbands, lovers, and children. Cotton's crimes were discovered in 1872, and she was convicted and executed by hanging in 1873.

Cotton was born on October 31, 1832, in the village of Low Moorsley, County Durham, England. She was the daughter of a colliery labourer and grew up in poverty. She received little formal education and started working as a nursemaid when she was a teenager.

Cotton married her first husband, William Mowbray, in 1852, and the couple had five children together. However, all of the children died in infancy, and Mowbray died in 1865, allegedly from an intestinal disorder.

After Mowbray's death, Cotton remarried several times, and all of her husbands and lovers died under suspicious circumstances. Her second husband, George Ward, died in 1866, leaving Cotton with two stepchildren. Her third husband, James Robinson, died in 1867, and Cotton received a small insurance payout from his death. She then married her fourth husband, Frederick Cotton, in 1870, and the couple had three children together. However, two of the children died in infancy, and Frederick Cotton died in 1871, allegedly from typhoid fever.

After Frederick's death, Cotton moved to West Auckland, County Durham, where she met and married her fifth husband, Joseph Nattrass, in 1872. Nattrass was a widower with five children, and Cotton became the stepmother to his children. However, Nattrass became suspicious of Cotton after several of his children became ill and died. He eventually forced her to leave the household, and Cotton moved to nearby Seaham Harbour.

The use of arsenic to murder husbands, lovers, and children

ARSENIC IS A HIGHLY toxic chemical that has been used as a murder weapon for centuries. It is tasteless, odorless, and easily available, making it a popular choice for those seeking to commit murder. In particular, arsenic was frequently used by women in the 19th century to kill their husbands, lovers, and even their own children. The following is a discussion of the use of arsenic as a murder weapon and its impact on society.

Arsenic is a naturally occurring element that can be found in rocks, soil, and water. It has been used for centuries for medicinal purposes, but it is also highly toxic and can cause a wide range of symptoms, including vomiting, diarrhea, convulsions, and death. In the 19th century, arsenic was readily available and was commonly used in household products such as wallpaper, insecticides, and rat poison.

EVIL WOMEN IN HISTORY: UNCOVERING THE GRUESOME CRIMES OF TEN NOTORIOUS FEMALE KILLERS

Women were particularly adept at using arsenic as a murder weapon. They often used small doses of the chemical over an extended period of time, so as not to arouse suspicion. This method of poisoning was known as "slow poisoning," and it was frequently used to kill husbands and lovers who were deemed to be unsatisfactory or inconvenient.

One of the most notorious female arsenic killers was Mary Ann Cotton, who was believed to have killed as many as 21 people, including her husbands, lovers, and children. Cotton was born in the northeast of England in 1832 and grew up in poverty. She was married at the age of 20 and had four children, but all of them died young. Cotton subsequently married three more times, and each of her husbands and several of her lovers died under mysterious circumstances.

Cotton's modus operandi was to take out life insurance policies on her victims before poisoning them with arsenic. She would then collect the insurance money and move on to her next victim. Cotton was eventually caught and tried for murder in 1873. She was found guilty and hanged the following year.

Another famous arsenic killer was Belle Gunness, an American woman who is believed to have killed as many as 40 people, including her husbands and suitors. Gunness was born in Norway in 1859 and immigrated to the United States in 1881. She married a fellow Norwegian immigrant, but he died under mysterious circumstances, and Gunness collected his life insurance money. She subsequently married two more men, both of whom also died under suspicious circumstances.

In addition to her husbands, Gunness also killed several suitors who responded to personal ads she had placed in newspapers seeking a "comely widow." Gunness would lure the men to her farm, where she would murder them and bury their bodies in her orchard. In 1908, a fire destroyed Gunness's farmhouse, and the remains of several men, including her last husband and their three children, were found in the rubble. Gunness herself was never found, leading to speculation that she had faked her own death and escaped.

The use of arsenic as a murder weapon had a profound impact on society. It led to an increased awareness of the dangers of toxic chemicals and prompted the development of new forensic techniques for detecting poison. It also highlighted the vulnerability of women in the 19th century, who often had few options for escaping unhappy marriages or abusive relationships.

The use of arsenic as a murder weapon by women in the 19th century was a dark chapter in history. It was a reflection of the limited options available to women at the time and the desire to exert control over their lives. The legacy of this period lives on in the public consciousness, as evidenced by the continued fascination with female arsenic killers and the use of poison as a plot device in literature and film.

Her arrest, trial, and execution

MARY ANN COTTON'S KILLING spree came to an end when she was arrested in West Auckland, County Durham, in 1872. The local doctor, Dr. Kilburn, became suspicious of her when three of her children died within a short period. The doctor noted that the children had similar symptoms, and he suspected that they had been poisoned.

After the exhumation of Mary Ann's daughter, the authorities discovered traces of arsenic in her body. Mary Ann was arrested and charged with murder. The police then began to investigate her past, and they discovered that several of her previous husbands and children had also died under suspicious circumstances.

Mary Ann Cotton's trial began on March 5, 1873, at Durham Assizes. She was charged with the murder of her son Charles Edward Cotton, who had died in 1872. She pleaded not guilty to the charge. The prosecution presented evidence from several witnesses who testified that Mary Ann had bought arsenic before Charles's death. They also presented evidence that Mary Ann had insured Charles's life for £10.

The defense argued that Charles had died of natural causes, and that Mary Ann had no motive to kill him. They also claimed that the arsenic found in his body could have been the result of the doctor's treatment. However, the jury found Mary Ann guilty, and she was sentenced to death.

After her conviction, Mary Ann confessed to killing 21 people, including her four husbands, her mother, several of her children, and a number of other people who had come into her life. She claimed that she had poisoned them with arsenic to collect their life insurance policies.

On March 24, 1873, Mary Ann Cotton was hanged at Durham County Gaol. Her execution was attended by a large crowd of people who had come to witness the event. Before she died, Mary Ann made a statement in which she denied any involvement in the murders. She claimed that she had been falsely accused and that the evidence against her was circumstantial.

Mary Ann Cotton's case has since become one of the most notorious in British criminal history. Her actions shocked the nation and sparked a national debate about the role of women in society. Some people saw her as a monster, while others saw her as a victim of circumstance.

The case also led to changes in the law regarding life insurance policies. Prior to Mary Ann's case, it was possible to insure anyone's life, regardless of their relationship to the policyholder. However, after her case, the law was changed to require that the policyholder must have an insurable interest in the life of the person they are insuring.

In popular culture, Mary Ann Cotton has been the subject of several books, films, and television programs. She has been portrayed as a cold-blooded killer, a tragic figure, and a feminist icon. Her case continues to fascinate and horrify people to this day.

Chapter 7: Ilse Koch

Her background and marriage to Karl Koch

Ilse Koch, also known as the "Bitch of Buchenwald," was a notorious Nazi war criminal who gained infamy for her role as the wife of Karl Koch, the commandant of the Buchenwald concentration camp in Germany. Born on September 22, 1906, in Dresden, Germany, Koch grew up in a middle-class family and was known for her beauty and charm. However, her life would take a dark turn as she became involved with the Nazi party and committed unspeakable atrocities during the Holocaust.

Koch's involvement with the Nazi party began in the 1930s when she joined the League of German Girls, a branch of the Hitler Youth. She quickly rose through the ranks and became a leader in the organization. In 1936, she met Karl Koch, a high-ranking SS officer, and they were married the following year. Karl Koch was later appointed as the commandant of the Buchenwald concentration camp in 1937, and Ilse Koch accompanied him to the camp.

Ilse Koch's role in the atrocities committed at Buchenwald is a subject of controversy and debate. Some reports allege that she was responsible for selecting prisoners to be killed and personally carried out horrific acts of torture and murder.

Others suggest that she was a willing accomplice to her husband's crimes and was complicit in the torture and killing of thousands of prisoners.

One of the most infamous accusations against Ilse Koch was that she had prisoners' skin made into lampshades, although this has been disputed by some historians. She was also known for her cruelty towards the prisoners, often using her whip to beat them, and for her sexual relationships with SS guards.

Karl Koch was arrested and executed in 1945, and Ilse Koch was taken into custody by American forces. She was tried by a military tribunal for war crimes and was found guilty of charges that included ordering the murder of prisoners and taking souvenirs from the bodies of executed prisoners. She was sentenced to life in prison and was imprisoned at several different facilities over the years, including Aichach, Landsberg, and Frankfurt prisons.

During her time in prison, Ilse Koch became known for her volatile personality and her attempts to manipulate the system to her advantage. She attempted suicide on several occasions and was involved in a number of fights with other prisoners. In 1951, she was found dead in her cell, having hanged herself with a bedsheet. Her death was initially ruled a suicide, but some have suggested that she may have been murdered by other prisoners.

The legacy of Ilse Koch is one of horror and cruelty, and her actions at Buchenwald continue to shock and disturb people to this day. Although the full extent of her involvement in the atrocities committed at the camp may never be known, her role as a willing accomplice to her husband's crimes and her personal acts of cruelty towards prisoners cannot be denied. Her story serves as a reminder of the dangers of blindly following extremist ideologies and the devastating consequences of unchecked power.

Her role in running Nazi concentration camps

ILSE KOCH, ALSO KNOWN as the "Bitch of Buchenwald," was a German woman who was married to Karl Koch, the commandant of the Buchenwald concentration camp. She played a significant role in the running of the camp and was known for her sadistic and cruel treatment of prisoners.

Koch was born in Dresden, Germany in 1906, and grew up in a middle-class family. She married Karl Koch in 1936, and soon after, he was appointed as the commandant of the newly established Buchenwald concentration camp. Koch quickly became involved in the running of the camp and was known for her brutal treatment of prisoners.

One of Koch's most notorious acts was her obsession with collecting the skin of prisoners who had tattoos. She would order the prisoners to be killed, and then their skin would be removed and sent to her to be made into lampshades, book covers, and other objects. It is estimated that she ordered the murder of hundreds of prisoners for this purpose.

Koch was also known for her cruel treatment of female prisoners, who she would often subject to sexual abuse and torture. She would personally select women for her "special treatment," and they would be taken to her private quarters, where they would be raped, beaten, and sometimes killed.

Koch's behavior was eventually reported to the SS authorities, and she was arrested in 1943 and charged with murder, abuse, and corruption. Her husband had already been arrested and executed for his role in the camp, and she was put on trial separately.

Koch's trial was highly publicized, and she was depicted in the media as a sadistic monster. She was found guilty of multiple charges and sentenced to life in prison. However, she was granted a retrial in 1951, and during the trial, she claimed that she had been forced to commit her crimes by her husband and that she was innocent.

Despite her claims of innocence, Koch was found guilty once again and sentenced to life in prison. She was held in several different prisons throughout her imprisonment and was reportedly treated harshly by her fellow inmates, who saw her as a symbol of the horrors of the Nazi regime.

Koch committed suicide in her cell in 1967, using a bedsheet to hang herself. Her legacy remains one of the most infamous examples of the cruelty and sadism of the Nazi concentration camp system.

The accusations of murder and cruelty

ILSE KOCH, ALSO KNOWN as the "Bitch of Buchenwald," was accused of heinous crimes during her time as the wife of Karl Koch, the commandant of the Buchenwald concentration camp in Nazi Germany. Born in Dresden, Germany in 1906, Koch was raised in a strict family with a military background. She worked as a secretary before marrying Karl Koch in 1936 and becoming a prominent figure in the Nazi Party.

After her husband was appointed commandant of the Buchenwald camp in 1937, Koch used her position to indulge in her sadistic desires. She was known to take pleasure in beating prisoners and ordering the deaths of those who displeased her. Koch was also obsessed with collecting human skin, which she had fashioned into lampshades and other household items. The true extent of her crimes is unknown, as much of the evidence was destroyed before she could be brought to trial.

After the war, Koch was arrested by the Allies and charged with crimes against humanity. She was accused of selecting prisoners for medical experiments, ordering the deaths of prisoners, and using her position to indulge her sadistic desires. One of the most notorious accusations against her was the use of human skin to create lampshades and other household items.

During her trial, Koch maintained her innocence and claimed that the accusations against her were fabricated. However, her behavior during the proceedings was erratic, and she was often seen laughing and mocking the testimony of survivors. Despite her protests, Koch was found guilty and sentenced to life in prison.

Koch's time in prison was marked by controversy and speculation. She was often accused of receiving preferential treatment from the guards and was rumored to have had affairs with them. In 1967, Koch was found dead in her cell, having committed suicide by hanging herself with a bedsheet. However, some conspiracy theories suggest that she may have been murdered by the guards or even escaped from prison and assumed a new identity.

The accusations against Ilse Koch are some of the most horrific to come out of the Nazi regime. Her sadistic behavior and obsession with human skin have made her a notorious figure in history, and her actions have been the subject of numerous books, movies, and other media. While the true extent of her crimes may never be known, Koch's legacy serves as a chilling reminder of the horrors that can arise when people in positions of power abuse their authority.

EVIL WOMEN IN HISTORY: UNCOVERING THE GRUESOME CRIMES OF TEN NOTORIOUS FEMALE KILLERS

Chapter 8: Irma Grese

Her background and employment as a guard at Nazi concentration camps

Irma Grese was a Nazi guard at several concentration camps during World War II, and is remembered as one of the most notorious female war criminals of the Nazi regime. Born on October 7, 1923, in Wrechen, Germany, she grew up in a rural family with six siblings. Her parents were strict and instilled in their children the importance of physical fitness and obedience to authority.

At the age of 15, Grese left school and began working as an assistant nurse in a hospital. However, she was fired after just a few months due to a poor work ethic and disciplinary issues. She then worked as a dairy maid on a farm, but left that job as well to join the SS in 1942 at the age of 19.

Grese began her career in the SS as a guard at Ravensbrück concentration camp, where she was assigned to work in the women's section. She was known for her cruelty and brutality towards the prisoners, and was promoted to a supervisory position within a year. In 1944, she was transferred to Auschwitz-Birkenau, where she was put in charge of a group of prisoners called the "Kanada Kommando," who were responsible for sorting the belongings of incoming prisoners. Grese was known to beat and whip prisoners, and was also accused of personally selecting women and children for the gas chambers.

In addition to her work at the concentration camps, Grese was also known for her relationships with several high-ranking Nazi officers, including Josef Mengele and Amon Goeth. She was even rumored to have had a sexual relationship with Goeth, who was the commandant of the Plaszow concentration camp.

In 1945, Grese was captured by British forces and put on trial for war crimes. During the trial, she was accused of committing numerous atrocities, including shooting prisoners for fun, setting dogs on them, and selecting prisoners for the gas chambers. She was found guilty and sentenced to death by hanging.

Her role in torture and murder of prisoners

IRMA GRESE WAS A FEMALE guard who worked at several Nazi concentration camps during World War II, including Ravensbrück, Auschwitz, and Bergen-Belsen. She is infamous for her role in the torture and murder of prisoners, particularly women and children, earning her the nickname "The Hyena of Auschwitz."

Irma Ida Ilse Grese was born on October 7, 1923, in Wrechen, a small village in the region of Mecklenburg, Germany. Her parents were both farmers, and Irma was the third of five children. She grew up in a strict household and was described as being a hardworking, obedient child. Her father died when she was 12, and her mother struggled to provide for the family.

In 1940, at the age of 17, Grese left home to work as a dairy maid in Ravensbrück, a concentration camp for women. There, she witnessed the brutal treatment of prisoners by the Nazi guards, but she was not deterred. Instead, she was inspired to join the SS, the paramilitary organization responsible for carrying out the Holocaust. In 1942, she was accepted into the SS and sent to Auschwitz-Birkenau, the largest of the Nazi concentration camps.

As a female guard, Grese was responsible for overseeing the women's camp at Auschwitz-Birkenau. She quickly gained a reputation for being sadistic and cruel, particularly towards the prisoners who were selected for the gas chambers. She took pleasure in beating and torturing prisoners and was known for her fondness for dogs, which she used to attack prisoners. She was also involved in selecting prisoners for medical experiments, many of which were designed to inflict maximum pain and suffering.

In 1944, Grese was transferred to Bergen-Belsen, where conditions were even worse than at Auschwitz. There, she oversaw the so-called "starvation bunker," a small, windowless building where prisoners were left to die of hunger and thirst. Grese was also involved in the selection and execution of prisoners and was known for her brutality towards women and children.

When the war ended in 1945, Grese was arrested by British forces and charged with war crimes. At her trial, witnesses testified to her sadistic behavior and involvement in the torture and murder of prisoners. She was found guilty and sentenced to death by hanging. On December 13, 1945, she was executed at Hamelin prison, becoming one of the youngest women to be executed under British law.

In the years since her death, Grese has become a symbol of the cruelty and brutality of the Nazi regime. Her story has been the subject of numerous books, films, and documentaries, and she continues to fascinate and horrify people around the world. Her role in the Holocaust serves as a reminder of the dangers of unchecked power and the need for vigilance against tyranny and oppression.

The trial, conviction, and execution

IRMA GRESE, ALSO KNOWN as the "Hyena of Auschwitz," was a female SS guard who served at several Nazi concentration camps during World War II. She was notorious for her sadistic behavior towards prisoners, including torture and murder. Grese was later captured, tried, and executed for her crimes.

Born in 1923 in Wrechen, Germany, Grese was the daughter of a dairy farmer. She ewas known to be a difficult child and had a tumultuous relationship with her father. At the age of 15, Grese joined the League of German Girls, the female youth organization of the Nazi Party. After completing her schooling, she worked as a nurse's assistant and later as a dairy maid.

In 1942, at the age of 19, Grese applied to join the SS, the Nazi Party's paramilitary organization. She was initially rejected but eventually accepted in June 1943 and was assigned to work as a guard at Ravensbrück concentration camp for women.

Grese quickly gained a reputation for her cruelty towards prisoners, often beating them with a whip or club. She was transferred to Auschwitz-Birkenau in 1943, where she was promoted to the rank of SS-Rapportführerin (SS report leader) and was responsible for selecting women and children for the gas chambers. She was also known to participate in medical experiments on prisoners.

Grese was transferred to Bergen-Belsen in 1944, where conditions were particularly horrific. She was put in charge of a group of women prisoners known as the "corridor of death," where she would beat and torture prisoners with a whip. She was also known to have selected prisoners for the gas chambers and to have participated in the burning of bodies in the camp's crematorium.

After the war ended, Grese was captured by British forces and put on trial at the Belsen Trial in 1945. She was charged with crimes against humanity and war crimes, including murder, torture, and participating in medical experiments on prisoners. During the trial, witnesses testified to Grese's sadistic behavior, including her selection of prisoners for the gas chambers and her participation in medical experiments.

Despite her defense team arguing that she was following orders, Grese was found guilty on all charges and sentenced to death. She was hanged at Hamelin prison on December 13, 1945, at the age of 22.

Irma Grese was a notorious SS guard who participated in the torture and murder of prisoners at several Nazi concentration camps during World War II. She gained a reputation for her sadistic behavior towards prisoners and was later captured, tried, and executed for her crimes. Her story serves as a reminder of the horrific atrocities committed during the Holocaust and the need to never forget the lessons of history.

EVIL WOMEN IN HISTORY: UNCOVERING THE GRUESOME CRIMES OF TEN NOTORIOUS FEMALE KILLERS

Chapter 9: Katherine Knight

Her background and relationships

Katherine Knight was an Australian woman born in 1955 who grew up in a small town in New South Wales. Her childhood was marked by violence and abuse, as her father was an alcoholic who regularly beat her mother and siblings. Despite this, Knight was known as a quiet and reserved child and showed a strong interest in animals and nature.

As a teenager, Knight had a brief relationship with a boy named David Kellett, who later became her husband. The couple had two daughters together before separating after four years of marriage. Following the split, Knight entered into a series of tumultuous relationships with men, some of whom were physically abusive.

Knight's most infamous relationship was with John Price, a man she met in 1995. Price was a father of three and a well-respected member of the community in Aberdeen, New South Wales. Despite his initial reservations, Price soon fell for Knight's charm and the couple began a relationship that would ultimately lead to his death.

Knight's relationship with Price was marked by violence and abuse. She was known to be possessive and jealous, often accusing him of cheating on her. On one occasion, she stabbed him in the chest with a pair of scissors, but he refused to press charges. In the months leading up to his death, Price expressed concern for his safety to friends and family, but did not seek help from the police.

On February 29, 2000, Knight brutally murdered Price in his home. She stabbed him multiple times with a butcher's knife and then skinned him, hanging his skin on a meat hook in the living room. She then decapitated Price and cooked parts of his body, intending to serve them to his children. Fortunately, Price's employer contacted the police after he failed to show up for work, and Knight was arrested at the scene of the crime.

Knight's trial was one of the most sensational in Australian history. She pleaded not guilty to murder, claiming that she had no memory of the event due to her history of alcohol abuse and blackouts. However, the evidence presented by the prosecution was overwhelming, and Knight was found guilty of murder and sentenced to life in prison without the possibility of parole.

Knight's crime shocked the nation and brought attention to the issue of domestic violence in Australia. In the years following her conviction, the government introduced stricter laws around domestic violence and the use of firearms. Knight remains in prison to this day, and her case continues to be a subject of fascination and horror for many.

Katherine Knight's background was marked by violence and abuse, and her relationships with men were often tumultuous and volatile. Her most infamous relationship with John Price ended in his brutal murder, which shocked Australia and brought attention to the issue of domestic violence. Knight's trial and conviction were highly publicized, and her crime continues to be a subject of fascination and horror.

The murder of partner and dismemberment of body

KATHERINE KNIGHT IS one of the most notorious female murderers in Australian history. Born on October 24, 1955, in Tenterfield, New South Wales, she had a troubled childhood marked by physical and sexual abuse. She was the youngest of four children, and her father was an abusive alcoholic. He would often rape her mother in front of the children and violently beat her. The family was also known for their violence towards animals, and Katherine was said to have been fascinated by blood and death from a young age.

Katherine had a tumultuous love life, having had numerous relationships with different men. In 1974, she married David Kellett, a co-worker at the abattoir where she worked. The marriage was short-lived, and the couple had a daughter before separating. She later had a long-term relationship with John Price, a co-worker at the abattoir, which would ultimately lead to her downfall.

On February 29, 2000, Katherine stabbed John Price 37 times with a butcher's knife before skinning him and hanging his skin on a meat hook in their living room. She then decapitated his head and cooked parts of his body, planning to serve them to his children. She also left a note on his body that read, "Time got you back Jonathan for rapping my daughter." This was a reference to an incident in which John's daughter accused him of sexually abusing her, but the allegations were never substantiated.

After the murder, Katherine attempted to take her own life by taking a large number of pills. However, she was discovered by police and taken to the hospital, where she recovered. She was later charged with the murder of John Price and faced a trial in October 2001.

During the trial, the prosecution argued that Katherine had committed the murder out of jealousy and revenge after John had kicked her out of their house. They also presented evidence of her history of violence and erratic behavior, including a previous incident in which she had stabbed another man and threatened to kill him. The defense tried to argue that Katherine had a history of mental illness and was not responsible for her actions.

Despite the defense's arguments, the jury found Katherine Knight guilty of murder, and she became the first woman in Australia to be sentenced to life imprisonment without the possibility of parole. In delivering the sentence, Justice Barry O'Keefe described the murder as "horrific and grotesque" and stated that Katherine had shown no remorse for her actions.

Katherine Knight's case has attracted significant media attention, with many describing her as one of the most violent and dangerous women in Australian history. Her story has been the subject of numerous documentaries, books, and even a feature film. She remains incarcerated at Silverwater Women's Correctional Centre in New South Wales.

Katherine Knight's troubled childhood, violent relationships, and mental instability all contributed to her committing one of the most horrific murders in Australian history. Her actions shocked the nation and led to her becoming one of the most notorious female killers of all time.

Her trial, conviction, and imprisonment

KATHERINE KNIGHT, ALSO known as the "Black Knight," is an Australian woman who was convicted of the gruesome murder of her partner, John Price. The crime was so brutal that it made headlines around the world, and Katherine became the first woman in Australia to receive a life sentence without parole.

Katherine Knight was born on October 24, 1955, in Tenterfield, New South Wales, Australia. She was the youngest of four children and was raised in a dysfunctional family environment. Her father, Jack Knight, was a violent and abusive alcoholic who frequently beat her mother and terrorized the children. Katherine was sexually abused by several family members, including her brothers and uncles, from a young age.

Despite the hardships of her childhood, Katherine was known as a bright and intelligent student. She was also an accomplished athlete, excelling in sports like netball and running. After finishing high school, she worked as a cutter at a meatworks and then as a butcher in a local abattoir.

Katherine's first marriage was to David Kellett, with whom she had two daughters. The marriage was violent and abusive, with both parties physically and emotionally abusing each other. They eventually separated, and Katherine moved on to a series of tumultuous relationships with various men.

In 1995, Katherine began dating John Price, a father of three who worked as a miner in Aberdeen, New South Wales. The relationship was marked by extreme jealousy, possessiveness, and violence. Katherine would fly into rages over minor issues, assaulting John and even stabbing him on one occasion. Despite this, John continued the relationship, perhaps because he feared what Katherine might do if he tried to leave her.

On February 29, 2000, after an argument, Katherine brutally murdered John Price in his home. She stabbed him at least 37 times with a large butcher knife, and then skinned him and hung his skin on a meat hook in the living room. She also decapitated him and cooked parts of his body, planning to serve them to his children.

Before Katherine could carry out her plan, the police arrived at the scene and arrested her. She was charged with murder and went to trial in October 2001. The trial was one of the most high-profile in Australian history, with gruesome details of the murder being recounted in the media. Katherine initially pleaded not guilty, claiming that she had no memory of the events due to a dissociative disorder. However, the jury rejected this defense, and Katherine was convicted of murder and sentenced to life imprisonment without parole.

Katherine Knight's trial and conviction were controversial, with some arguing that she should have been found not guilty due to her alleged mental illness. However, others argued that her crime was so heinous that she deserved the harshest possible punishment. Regardless of where one falls on this debate, it is clear that Katherine Knight's crime was one of the most gruesome and disturbing in Australian history.

In prison, Katherine has reportedly shown little remorse for her crime. She has been involved in several violent incidents with other inmates and prison guards and has even swallowed razor blades and other objects in attempts to harm herself. Despite this, she remains behind bars and is unlikely to ever be released.

EDWARD TURNER

Chapter 10: Elizabeth Bathory

Her background and wealth

Elizabeth Bathory, also known as the "Blood Countess," was a Hungarian noblewoman born in 1560. She was born into one of the most prominent families in Hungary, the Bathory family, which was one of the wealthiest families in the country. Bathory grew up in the family's castle, Ecsed Castle, and was raised in the Catholic faith.

Bathory was educated in the sciences and learned several languages, including Hungarian, Latin, and German. She was also trained in sword fighting and horseback riding. At the age of 15, Bathory married Ferenc Nadasdy, a fellow nobleman. The couple had five children together and Bathory became known for her beauty and intelligence.

During the 17th century, rumors began to circulate about Bathory's behavior. According to legend, Bathory was said to have tortured and killed young girls in her castle, and then bathed in their blood to maintain her youth and beauty. The exact number of victims is unknown, but it is believed to be between 80 and 650.

Bathory was eventually arrested in 1610 after complaints from the families of the missing girls reached the authorities. An investigation was launched, and Bathory's servants were brought in for questioning. Several of them confessed to helping Bathory torture and kill young girls.

Bathory herself was not put on trial, as she was a noblewoman and it was believed that a public trial would bring shame to her family. Instead, she was placed under house arrest in her castle. She remained there until her death in 1614, at the age of 54.

The exact nature of Bathory's crimes is still debated by historians. Some believe that she was a sadistic killer who enjoyed torturing and killing young girls, while others believe that she was the victim of a political conspiracy designed to destroy her family's reputation.

Regardless of the truth, Bathory has become one of the most infamous figures in history, with her legend inspiring numerous works of literature, film, and music. Her name has become synonymous with cruelty and violence, and she remains a subject of fascination and horror to this day.

The accusations of torturing and killing young girls

ELIZABETH BATHORY, also known as the "Blood Countess," was a noblewoman who lived in the Kingdom of Hungary in the late 16th and early 17th centuries. She is infamous for the accusations of torturing and killing numerous young girls, many of whom were her own servants, in order to bathe in their blood and maintain her youth and beauty.

Born into a powerful and wealthy family in 1560, Bathory was raised in a castle in Hungary. Her family was known for their military prowess and had a long history of involvement in politics and governance in the region. Bathory was well-educated and fluent in several languages, including Hungarian, Slovak, German, and Latin.

At the age of 15, Bathory married Ferenc Nadasdy, a fellow nobleman who was known for his military victories against the Ottoman Turks. Together, they had four children, and Bathory became the lady of the Csejte Castle, a property that was gifted to her by her husband. Nadasdy spent much of his time away from home, leaving Bathory in charge of managing the estate and caring for their children.

It was during this time that Bathory's reputation began to take a dark turn. It was said that she would often beat her servants, sometimes to the point of death, and that she would use needles to prick and torture them. She also reportedly engaged in sexual relationships with both men and women, including her own servants.

In the early 1600s, rumors began to circulate about Bathory's gruesome acts of violence. According to the stories, Bathory believed that bathing in the blood of virgins would keep her youthful and beautiful. She allegedly lured young girls to her castle with the promise of work or education, and then subjected them to horrific torture and murder.

The accusations against Bathory were initially brought to the attention of the authorities by a Lutheran minister named Istvan Magyari, who claimed that he had witnessed Bathory killing girls in the castle. He wrote to the King of Hungary, Matthias II, and urged him to investigate the matter.

In December 1610, King Matthias sent two notaries to Csejte Castle to investigate the accusations against Bathory. They reportedly found the bodies of several girls who had been beaten, burned, and mutilated. Bathory was arrested along with several of her accomplices, including her two most trusted servants, Dorka and Helena.

Bathory's trial was held in January 1611. Because of her noble status, she was not subjected to torture, unlike her accomplices. Nevertheless, the evidence against her was overwhelming, and she was found guilty of 80 counts of murder.

Because of her status as a noblewoman, Bathory was not executed for her crimes. Instead, she was sentenced to life imprisonment in her own castle. She was walled up in a set of rooms, with only a small opening through which food and water could be passed. She died there in 1614 at the age of 54.

The exact number of victims of Elizabeth Bathory's crimes is not known, but it is believed to be between 30 and 60 young girls. Her legacy has become a symbol of both the brutal violence that can be perpetrated by those in positions of power and the dangers of unchecked vanity and obsession with youth and beauty. Bathory's story has been the subject of numerous books, films, and other works of art over the years, cementing her place in history as one of the most notorious female serial killers of all time.

The trial and imprisonment

ELIZABETH BATHORY, also known as the "Blood Countess," was a Hungarian noblewoman born in 1560. She came from a wealthy and influential family and was married to Ferenc Nadasdy, a soldier and member of another wealthy family. The couple had four children together and lived in the Castle Cachtice, in present-day Slovakia.

Bathory was notorious for her cruelty, particularly towards young girls. She was accused of torturing and killing dozens of young girls, with some estimates putting the number at over 650 victims. She was known to have believed that bathing in the blood of young girls would preserve her youth and beauty.

The accusations against Bathory began in 1602 when a Lutheran minister named Istvan Magyari accused her of torturing and killing young girls. Magyari reported that he had been approached by the parents of a girl named Pola, who had disappeared after working at Bathory's castle. Magyari searched the castle and found several girls who had been severely beaten and injured. Bathory was arrested and charged with witchcraft, murder, and other crimes.

Bathory's trial began in 1610, but due to her status as a noblewoman, she was not subjected to the usual legal proceedings. Instead, the trial was held in secret, and Bathory was kept in a room in her castle during the proceedings. She was not allowed to have a lawyer or defend herself in court.

Despite the lack of a proper trial, Bathory was found guilty of torture and murder, and her accomplices were also convicted.

Bathory was sentenced to life imprisonment, and her accomplices were either executed or imprisoned.

Bathory was kept in solitary confinement in her castle, and her windows were bricked up to prevent her from communicating with anyone outside. She was allowed to receive food and water through a small hole in the wall. Bathory remained in confinement for four years until her death in 1614.

The story of Elizabeth Bathory has captured the imaginations of people for centuries, and her legend has grown over time. Some have even suggested that she may have inspired the fictional character of Dracula, although there is little evidence to support this claim.

In recent years, historians and scholars have cast doubt on the accuracy of the accusations against Bathory. Some have suggested that Bathory may have been the victim of a political conspiracy, or that she was falsely accused by her enemies. Others have argued that Bathory's alleged crimes were exaggerated and distorted over time.

Despite the uncertainty surrounding the details of Bathory's life and the accusations against her, her story continues to fascinate and intrigue people to this day. The legend of the "Blood Countess" is a reminder of the dark side of human nature and the enduring power of myth and legend.

Conclusion

Throughout history, there have been many notorious female killers who have committed heinous crimes. Some of them were driven by financial gain, others by their sadistic tendencies, and some by their thirst for power. In this essay, we will compare the crimes of some of the most infamous female killers, including Belle Gunness, Mary Ann Cotton, Katherine Knight, and Elizabeth Bathory.

Belle Gunness was a Norwegian-American serial killer who murdered several men, women, and children for financial gain. She would lure her victims to her farm in Indiana, where she would kill them and bury their bodies. Her victims included her two husbands, suitors, and children. She was known to be a large woman, over six feet tall and weighing around 200 pounds, and she used her size and strength to overpower her victims. Gunness was never caught, and it is believed that she faked her own death in a fire to escape justice.

Mary Ann Cotton was a Victorian-era Englishwoman who poisoned several husbands, lovers, and children for financial gain. She would use arsenic to poison her victims, and it is estimated that she killed up to 21 people, including three of her husbands, several of her children, and her mother. She was finally caught and hanged in 1873.

Katherine Knight was an Australian woman who murdered her partner and dismembered his body. She had a history of violent behavior and was known to be very possessive of her partners. She killed her partner by stabbing him several times, then skinning him and cooking parts of his body. She placed his head in a pot on the stove, with vegetables and gravy. Knight was found guilty of murder and sentenced to life in prison without parole.

Elizabeth Bathory was a Hungarian countess who was accused of torturing and killing young girls in the late 16th and early 17th centuries. It is estimated that she killed hundreds of girls, and she was known for her sadistic tendencies. She would often beat, burn, and bite her victims before killing them. Bathory was never formally tried for her crimes but was confined to her castle until her death.

While these women committed different crimes, they all had several things in common. Firstly, they all had a history of violent behavior and tendencies. Secondly, they were all able to use their positions of power or manipulation skills to carry out their crimes. Lastly, they all showed a lack of empathy or remorse for their actions.

Another common thread among these women is that they all managed to escape justice for a time. Belle Gunness was never caught and is believed to have faked her own death to escape. Mary Ann Cotton was caught only after years of poisoning her victims. Katherine Knight was caught after her brutal murder of her partner. Elizabeth Bathory was never formally tried for her crimes and remained confined to her castle.

EVIL WOMEN IN HISTORY: UNCOVERING THE GRUESOME CRIMES OF TEN NOTORIOUS FEMALE KILLERS

These women are examples of some of the most notorious female killers in history. While their crimes were different, they all displayed a lack of empathy and used their positions of power or manipulation skills to carry out their heinous acts. Their ability to escape justice for a time is also a common thread among them. These women serve as a reminder of the dark side of human nature and the devastating impact that violent behavior can have on society.

The actions of the women discussed in this series of writings have had a profound impact on history. From the murders committed by Mary Ann Cotton in the 19th century to the atrocities committed by Ilse Koch and Irma Grese in Nazi concentration camps during World War II, their actions have left a lasting mark on the collective memory of humanity.

One common thread that runs through all of these stories is the way in which these women used their positions of power to inflict harm on those around them. Whether it was using their nursing skills to poison children, as in the case of Beverly Allitt, or their status as wives and lovers to murder their partners, as in the case of Katherine Knight, these women exploited the trust of those around them for their own gain.

Another common theme is the use of violence and cruelty. Elizabeth Bathory, for example, is believed to have tortured and killed as many as 650 young girls over a period of several years. Meanwhile, Ilse Koch was notorious for her sadistic treatment of prisoners at Buchenwald and Majdanek concentration camps, where she was known to have had prisoners killed for the purpose of using their skin to make lampshades and other items.

Despite the differences in their methods and motives, what these women share is a willingness to inflict harm on others without remorse or regard for the consequences. They represent a dark aspect of human nature that is all too often ignored or denied, and their actions serve as a reminder of the importance of vigilance and accountability in the face of evil.

Moreover, the impact of their crimes goes beyond the immediate victims and their families. The stories of these women have become part of the cultural memory, influencing literature, film, and popular culture. Elizabeth Bathory, for example, has been the subject of countless books and films, while the Nazi atrocities committed by Ilse Koch and Irma Grese have been documented in numerous historical studies and memoirs.

Ultimately, the stories of these women serve as a cautionary tale, a reminder of the dangers of unchecked power, cruelty, and the darker aspects of human nature. While we may never fully understand the motivations behind their actions, their stories serve as a warning that evil can come in many forms, and that it is up to us to remain vigilant against its insidious influence.

The concept of evil is one that has fascinated and perplexed humanity throughout history. It has been the subject of countless philosophical and theological debates, and it continues to be a topic of great interest in the modern era. In this final reflection, I will share my thoughts on the concept of evil.

Firstly, I believe that evil is a complex and multifaceted concept. It cannot be reduced to a simple definition or a set of characteristics. Evil can manifest itself in many different ways, ranging from petty acts of cruelty to large-scale atrocities that impact entire societies. Evil can also be driven by a variety of factors, including greed, jealousy, fear, or a desire for power.

Secondly, I believe that the concept of evil is deeply intertwined with our understanding of morality. In many cultures, evil is seen as the opposite of good, and the two are often thought of as complementary forces that exist in balance. This duality can be seen in many religious traditions, where evil is often personified as a devil or demon, while good is embodied by a god or other benevolent entity.

Thirdly, I believe that the existence of evil poses significant challenges for our understanding of the world. If evil is a fundamental part of human nature or the universe itself, then it raises questions about the nature of free will, the role of suffering in human life, and the possibility of a just and moral world.

Finally, I believe that our response to evil is a critical aspect of how we define ourselves as individuals and as a society. Whether we choose to confront evil head-on or turn a blind eye to its existence can have profound consequences for our own moral development and the well-being of others.

The concept of evil is a complex and multifaceted one that continues to challenge our understanding of the world and ourselves. While we may never fully comprehend the nature of evil, it is essential that we continue to engage with this concept and strive to confront and overcome it in all its forms.

Also by Edward Turner

Ghosts of Paris: Ten Haunted Places in the City of Love
Appalachian Nightmares: The Top 10 Creepy Creatures of the
Mountains
Asia's Top Ten Cryptids: Legends, Sightings, and Theories
Evil Women in History: Uncovering the Gruesome Crimes of
Ten Notorious Female Killers
Ghosts of London: Ten Haunted Places in The City
Ghosts of New York: Ten Haunted Places in The Big Apple
Missouri Nightmares: The Top 10 Chilling Legends
North America's Top Ten Cryptids: Legends, Sightings, and
Theories

About the Author

Edward Turner is a renowned author who specializes in exploring the realms of ghosts, the paranormal, and cryptids. With a captivating writing style and an insatiable curiosity for the unknown, Turner has garnered a dedicated following of readers who are captivated by his thrilling and eerie tales.

Born with an innate fascination for the supernatural, Turner has spent decades delving into the depths of paranormal phenomena, unearthing captivating stories and untangling mysteries that lie beyond the veil of the ordinary. His extensive research and meticulous attention to detail have earned him a reputation as a leading authority in the field.

Through his books, Turner expertly weaves together chilling accounts of encounters with ghosts, offering readers a glimpse into the ethereal world that coexists alongside our own. His ability to paint vivid portraits of spectral apparitions and convey the haunting atmosphere of haunted locations has made his works both spine-tingling and thought-provoking.

Turner's exploration of the paranormal doesn't stop at ghosts. He also dives into the fascinating world of cryptids—creatures that defy conventional explanation. His in-depth investigations into legendary creatures such as Bigfoot, the Loch Ness Monster, and the Chupacabra showcase his commitment to shedding light on these enigmatic beings.

With each page, Edward Turner's readers are drawn deeper into the enigmatic and unknown. His unique storytelling ability combined with his meticulous research has made him a sought-after author for those with an insatiable thirst for the supernatural. Whether delving into ghostly encounters or unraveling the mysteries of elusive cryptids, Turner's books offer a spine-chilling and immersive reading experience that leaves readers questioning the boundaries of our reality.

Edward Turner's works have earned critical acclaim and numerous accolades within the paranormal genre. He continues to explore the unexplained, captivating readers with his distinctive narrative style and unwavering dedication to unveiling the mysteries that lie hidden in the shadows.